EDGE BOOKS

X-SPORTS
EXTREME DIVING

BY KIM COVERT

CONSULTANT:
CAPTAIN CLIFF SCHMIDT
SCHMIDT MARINE SPECIALTIES INC.

Capstone press
Mankato, Minnesota

Edge Books are published by Capstone Press,
151 Good Counsel Drive, P.O. Box 669, Mankato, Minnesota 56002.
www.capstonepress.com

Library of Congress Cataloging-in-Publication Data
Covert, Kim.
   Extreme diving / by Kim Covert.
   p. cm. -- (Edge books, X-sports)
   Includes bibliographical references and index.
   ISBN 0-7368-3782-5 (hardcover)
   1. Diving--Juvenile literature. 2. Cave diving--Juvenile literature. 3. Skin diving--
Juvenile literature. I. Title. II. Series.
GV838.613.C68 2005
797.2--dc22   2004021610

Summary: Discusses types of extreme diving, including cave diving, ice diving, and
freediving, and the equipment and safety gear needed.

Editorial Credits
Connie Colwell Miller, editor; Jason Knudson, set designer; Enoch Peterson and
   Linda Clavel, book designers; Jason D. Miller, illustrator; Jo Miller,
   photo researcher; Scott Thoms, photo editor

Photo Credits
Cover: Corbis/Stephen Frink, diver with an underwater scooter

Aurora Photos/Randy Olson, 8
Corbis, 29; Amos Nachoum, 11, 13; Galen Rowell, 25; Jeffrey L. Rotman, 15;
   Reuters, 5; Rick Price, 22, 23; Stephen Frink, 7; Sygma/Franco Origlia, 27
Getty Images Inc./Time Life Pictures/Harley Soltes, 20
Index Stock Imagery/Volvox, 19

1 2 3 4 5 6 10 09 08 07 06 05

TABLE OF CONTENTS

CHAPTER 1

EXTREME DIVING

Tanya Streeter prepares to dive into the ocean. She steps onto a heavy sled that is attached to a cable. Streeter crosses her arms across a bar on the sled. She takes several deep breaths. She nods to her husband to release the sled.

Streeter rides the sled down the cable for two minutes. The sled stops when it's 175 yards (160 meters) below the surface of the water. Streeter has traveled the length of almost two football fields. Streeter blows a kiss to an underwater camera to record that she reached that depth.

LEARN ABOUT:
- Tanya Streeter
- Scuba diving
- Scuba training

On August 17, 2002, Tanya Streeter dove below the water almost the length of two football fields.

Streeter reaches up and inflates an airbag on the sled. It quickly brings her up to the surface. Streeter took three minutes, 26 seconds to complete her dive.

Streeter set the new world record for no-limits freediving. Streeter went 175 yards (160 meters) below the surface while holding her breath. She broke the women's and the men's world records. Many people believe this was the first time a woman beat a men's world record in any sport.

Freediving is a form of extreme diving. People who dive in caves and under ice are also extreme divers. Ice and cave divers are called technical divers. They learn how to dive in dangerous conditions.

SCUBA DIVING EQUIPMENT

Cave and ice divers use scuba equipment. Scuba stands for self-contained underwater breathing apparatus. Scuba equipment gives divers a supply of air to breathe. This air allows them to stay underwater for a long time.

Scuba equipment gives divers a supply of air to breathe under the surface of the water.

The hose regulator allows a diver to breathe air from the air tank.

8

Scuba divers carry an air tank. A single hose regulator is attached to the tank. The regulator allows divers to breathe air from the tank.

Divers often wear full body wet suits to protect them underwater. Divers also wear a Buoyancy Compensator Device (BCD). The BCD helps divers float underwater and avoid coral reefs. Divers wear a face mask or goggles. They wear fins on their feet to help them swim.

Divers carry other equipment to help them dive safely. A depth gauge measures how deeply they are swimming. The divers can tell how much air is left in a tank with a pressure gauge.

SCUBA DIVING TRAINING

People take classes to learn to scuba dive. This training can be completed in a few days.

Most scuba diving schools offer junior certification for ages 10 to 15. At age 15, divers can become certified as an open water diver.

CHAPTER 2

CAVE DIVING

Cave divers are explorers. They can find beautiful formations in underwater caverns and caves. A cavern is the entrance area of a cave that receives light from the surface of the water. In 1954, a group of divers found bones while diving in a cavern at Wakulla Springs in Florida. Scientists believe that the bones were from a creature that lived more than 10,000 years ago.

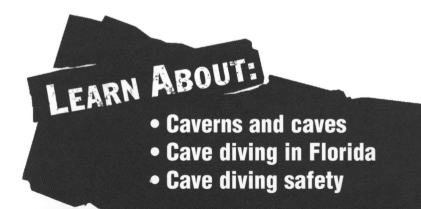

LEARN ABOUT:

- Caverns and caves
- Cave diving in Florida
- Cave diving safety

Cave divers explore caves where little light shines.

About Cave Diving

Some people call cave diving the most dangerous sport in the world. Since 1960, about 500 divers have died in cave diving accidents in North America. Cave divers can't swim straight up to the surface. They must swim out of a cave before going up. It's easy to get lost in the dark tunnels. Divers must save enough air in their tanks to reach the surface.

Many of the world's cave divers learn to dive in north-central Florida. They explore underwater limestone formations in Florida's caves. The remains of ancient sea creatures created these rock formations. Jackson Blue is a beautiful cave for divers to explore in Florida. The Devil's Eye cave system is another popular cave in Florida. Divers have mapped more than 30,000 feet (9,140 meters) of passageways in this cave.

Cave divers explore remains of ancient sea creatures in rock formations.

TRAINING AND EQUIPMENT

Cave divers need special training and certification. Most cave diving deaths occur because the divers were not properly prepared. Divers must be at least 18 years old to be certified. Cave diving is one of the most advanced diving certifications.

Cave divers need equipment to help them safely explore and get out of caves. They must carry a light to help them see in the caves. They carry two backup lights. Cave divers are also tied to a guideline. They bring this nylon rope into the cave with them. They can follow the guideline out of the cave and back to the surface. They also attach arrows to their guidelines to point the way to the nearest exit.

EDGE FACT

Divers sometimes use motor-powered scooters called Diver Propulsion Vehicles to travel underwater.

Cave divers learn to swim carefully through caves. They must be careful not to disturb the formations in the caves. They also do not want to touch the bottom of the cave, which can stir up silt. This clay-like substance makes the water cloudy.

GEAR DIAGRAM

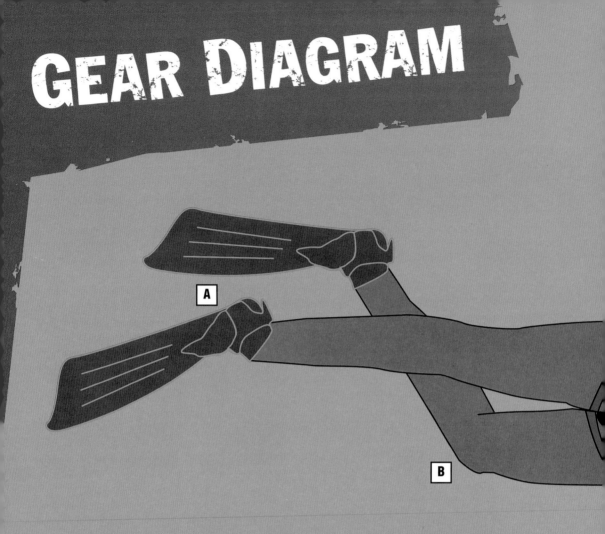

A Fins help divers push through the water.

B A wet suit keeps a diver's body warm.

C The air tank gives the diver a supply of air to breathe while underwater.

D The depth gauge tells the diver how far below the surface the diver has traveled.

E The regulator brings a supply of air from the air tank to the diver.

F Divers wear a face mask so they can see underwater.

CHAPTER 3

ICE DIVING

Many scuba divers want to explore new territory. Diving under the ice lets them dive in cold locations. Ice divers spot a variety of sea life in the clear water. Divers can see about 400 feet (122 meters) in cold water. In warm water, algae and other tiny creatures can make the water cloudy.

LEARN ABOUT:

- Ice diving teams
- Fun under the ice
- Underwater exploration

Ice divers enjoy beautiful sights in the cold, clear water.

Ice divers work in teams to help keep each other safe.

ABOUT ICE DIVING

For ice diving, ice should be at least
6 inches (15 centimeters) thick. Diving teams
prepare the ice for the dive. They usually cut a
triangle-shaped hole. They clear snow away
from the ice around the hole to let more light
into the water.

Ice divers work in teams of at least six
people. Ice diving teams include the diver
and line tenders. Line tenders hold on to a
safety line connected to the diver. Ice diving
teams must have a standby diver. This diver
waits at the surface, with all equipment ready.
This diver is ready to dive during an emergency.

EDGE FACT

About 10,000 ice divers in the
United States are certified by
the Professional Association of
Diving Instructors.

A safety line keeps each ice diver attached to the surface. This line is held into the ice with a large screw. The line tenders can pull on this line to bring a diver back up to the surface.

Ice divers take turns going into the water. They do not stay underwater as long as warm water divers. The water temperatures are usually just above freezing, or about 34 degrees Fahrenheit (1 degree Celsius).

Ice divers can explore the habitats of animals such as seals.

Ice divers can have fun under the ice. They watch their air bubbles float up and hit the ice. Sometimes they turn themselves upside down and walk along the ice under the surface of the water.

Ice divers in the Arctic and Antarctic regions dive along the edges of glaciers. They can explore the habitats of penguins, seals, and whales. Ice divers see colorful sea life on the ocean floor. They can explore ice caves within glaciers.

Equipment and Training

Ice divers need equipment and clothing to keep them safe underwater. They must have regulators that run in cold water. Each diver must carry a second air supply. They also wear a harness under their BCDs. The safety line attaches to this harness.

Ice divers dress for the cold air and water temperatures. They wear dry suits. These suits fit more loosely than wet suits. Divers often wear warm clothing under the dry suits. They also wear a hood and hand coverings.

Ice divers wear dry suits, hoods, and hand coverings to keep them warm under the ice.

Divers must be 18 years old to receive ice diving certification. They learn how to conserve the air in their tanks. They want to use only one-third of their air for diving down. They use another third to come back to the surface. Smart ice divers save one-third for emergencies.

CHAPTER 4

FREEDIVING

People have been freediving for thousands of years. Freedivers do not use breathing gear. Freediving is a growing sport in North America and around the world.

Freediving is very dangerous. Water pressure affects divers as they go deeper. This pressure squeezes their lungs to the size of oranges. Their heart rates can slow to less than 20 beats a minute.

FREEDIVING COMPETITIONS

The Association for the International Development of Apnea (AIDA) sets rules for international freediving competitions. In 2004, more than 130 freedivers competed in the 4th AIDA Freediving World Championships in Vancouver, Canada.

LEARN ABOUT:

- Freediving competitions
- Ballast
- Shallow water blackout

Some freedivers use weighted sleds to travel underwater.

AIDA has eight categories of freediving for world records and competitions. Constant weight freedivers dive down by swimming. The divers return to the surface the same way. In some competitions, these divers wear fins to help them go faster.

Freedivers can also compete in constant weight without fins. This category is very difficult. The divers descend without fins or other equipment to help them go down. The diver goes both down and back up by pulling on a rope.

Variable weight is another category of competitive freediving. Divers can use ballast to help them go down faster. This weight can be up to one-third of their body weight. They also wear fins to help them dive down faster. They must swim or climb a rope to come back up to the surface.

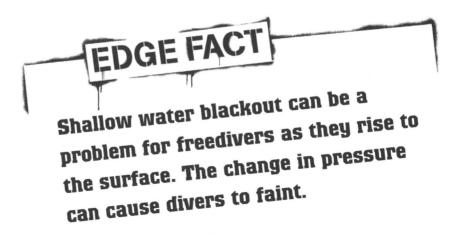

EDGE FACT

Shallow water blackout can be a problem for freedivers as they rise to the surface. The change in pressure can cause divers to faint.

The final competitive freediving category is called no-limits freediving. No-limits freedivers use a weighted sled that runs down a steel cable. When divers reach their bottom depth, they inflate an airbag to bring them to the surface.

Different types of extreme divers use different methods to dive. All extreme divers explore the wonders of the underwater world.

Constant weight freedivers descend using only a rope to guide them.

GLOSSARY

algae (AL-jee)—small plants that grow in water

ballast (BAL-uhst)—any heavy material that adds weight to an object

gauge (GAYJ)—an instrument for measuring something; divers use gauges to measure water pressure and depth.

glacier (GLAY-shur)—a large, slow-moving sheet of ice

limestone (LIME-stohn)—a hard rock formed from the remains of ancient sea creatures

regulator (REG-yoo-lay-tuhr)—a piece of equipment that allows divers to breathe air from an air tank

scuba (SKOO-buh)—self-contained underwater breathing apparatus; divers use scuba gear to allow them to breathe underwater.

silt (SILT)—small particles of soil that settle at the bottom of a river, lake, or ocean

Read More

Bailer, Darice. *Dive!: Your Guide to Snorkeling, Scuba, Night-Diving, Freediving, Exploring Shipwrecks, Caves, and More.* Extreme Sports. Washington, DC: National Geographic Society, 2002.

Earle, Sylvia A. *Dive!: My Adventures in the Deep Frontier.* Washington, DC: National Geographic Society, 1999.

Matsen, Bradford. *An Extreme Dive under the Antarctic Ice.* Incredible Deep-Sea Adventures. Berkeley Heights, N.J.: Enslow, 2003.

Internet Sites

FactHound offers a safe, fun way to find Internet sites related to this book. All of the sites on FactHound have been researched by our staff.

Here's how:

1. Visit *www.facthound.com*
2. Type in this special code **0736837825** for age-appropriate sites. Or enter a search word related to this book for a more general search.
3. Click on the **Fetch It** button.

FactHound will fetch the best sites for you!

INDEX